# BLUE FLAME

Emily Pettit

Carnegie Mellon University Press
Pittsburgh 2019

# Acknowledgments

Thank you to the editors of the following publications, where some of these poems first appeared:

Academy of American Poets Poem-a-Day Series: "A Fox's Tail Is Called a Brush"; *Boaat*: "Hands Like Lighters"; *Bomblog*: "A Name That Haunts You Your Name That Haunts You"; *Bone Bouquet*: "Object in Our Conscience"; *Clinic*: "After Vision" and "That That That"; *Fence*: "Water I Have Seen a Duck"; *Forklift, Ohio*: "The Eye of the Fly"; *GlitterPony*: "Hostile and Aggressive Feelings," "There Is Something Human About Wanting to Hold a Fork That Size," "The Heart Is My Favorite Organ but Not Because It Is Grand," "All of the Animals Were There" and "Keep Your Face Away from My Face"; *Ink Node*: "Because You Can Have This Idea About Being Afraid of Something"; *La Petite Zine*: "To Leave Half a Mind Is a Gift You Sometimes Give Yourself"; *NOÖ Journal*: "We Are Hearing the Loudest Animal Be Its Loudest"; *Oakland Review*: "Bug," "Indignant," "Tiny" (originally published under the title "Mad Tiny") and "The Opposition of Objects"; *Open Letters*: "I Am Asking You to Look at Me, Touch Me, Talk to Me"; *Propeller Magazine*: "They Will Call You Different Things"; *Sixth Finch*: "Lego Lady You Have Two Heads"; *thethepoetry blog*: "An Agreement Requires an Offer and Acceptance"; *The Undertow Review*: "Familiar Qualities We Admire"; *Vinyl Poetry*: "After Calming Down You Have an Old Feeling" and "You Keep Asking What I Want and I Don't Know What I Want"

Thank you to Jeff Alessandrelli and Bret Shepard at Dikembe Press for publishing some of these poems in the chapbook *Because You Can Have This Idea About Being Afraid of Something*.

Thank you Rachel B. Glaser, Kevin González, Mark Leidner, Dara Wier, and Michael Flanary.

Book design by Isabel McCarthy

Library of Congress Control Number 2018955997
ISBN 978-0-88748-648-7

10  9  8  7  6  5  4  3  2  1

# BLUE FLAME

## Books by Emily Pettit

*Goat in the Snow*
*Blue Flame*

*for Mike*

# Contents

## I.

# II.

# III.

*By Chivalries as tiny,*
*A Blossom, or a Book,*
*The seeds of smiles are planted—*
*Which blossom in the dark.*

—Emily Dickinson

I.

# OBJECT IN OUR CONSCIENCE

I heard a shark. It sounded like shock.
The noise the water makes. The noise
the shark makes the water make.
Your eyes rise from the sea.
The sea from a story you know not.
We can dance later and later.
Take the wrong risks later.
I would like to display gratitude for
encouragement now. Thank you
for liking my face in your dream.
To display gratitude for encouragement,
simply do anything. Hello everybody.
Break in. Cheer and clap. Throw your eyes
off. Mom's on the radio again.
You want to go into the structure
and for the structure to love you.
For it to be warm in the structure
and full of love. Full of geometry
and innovation. Like how our heads hide
the water. Like how our heads hide the water
that is in our head.

# BECAUSE YOU CAN HAVE THIS IDEA
# ABOUT BEING AFRAID OF SOMETHING

It is not an answer I am mapping. A definite
and timely expression of acceptance.
The burn bags are missing and what can this
mean? Error and ignorance are often fatal.
Or is it blissful? To wish to become an underwater
dune simply by wishing to become an underwater
dune. This is one of many thoughts inspired by
watching a stream meander over a beach, towards
the sea. We have no direction. We are damn serious
about not changing direction. Why wish to become
an underwater dune? They keep building up,
steeper and steeper, moving backwards against
the current until there is a rush and they dissolve
into turbulence. Of course, then they build again.
Part of our tradition is a fascination with simple
systems. Disruptive emotion, it's disruptive.
This is a simple observation. Like looking at
the palm. What is it saying about the future?
Look at the palm. It's history and your eyes.
Like geometric hallucinations. Like holding a sharp
edge. Like the science of functioning. To determine
nothing and move forward.

# I AM ASKING YOU TO LOOK AT ME, TOUCH ME, TALK TO ME

I have this to say, *Something was going to happen
and then it did.* Our gestures exceeded
the speed of light. They were practical
efforts. Practical efforts, such as raising chickens.
Such as standing and standing. Processing
information in your sleep. When you build
a fire in the snow it's a speculative treatment
of certain problems. I feel better when I feel
better. Let me explain the agreement. Or else
you explain impossible colors. Impossible
colors are a catastrophic visual failure
and not impossible. Not a ship sinking. A shore
out of shape. Some things will get lost. A neck.
The circle running. A true yellow blue.
There are always competing signals from one
system to another. There are options regarding
the ice. We can lick it or cross it. Further information
when you want it. Information always blinking.
A chime that rang. I fluctuate by night. I fluctuate
by night. In my head is a station where you
practice landing.

# THE EYE OF THE FLY

The eye of the fly is made of countless windows.
This place is in the process of becoming
a different place. Someone pulls out a chart.
There is a plan to build a beautiful city
and the plan gets seriously confused.
Steel implied and rung systems stumbling.
Bone implied and tender systems stumbling.
We attempt to draw things to scale. We are not
merciless. We are hopeful. We have a periscope
and we decide to use it. We experience taboo leaps
of the heart. Our displeasure is always delicate
until it starts to damage. The building
is always gentle until it starts to burn. The eye
of the fly, when seen up close, is scarred.
And we are scarred, the city scarred.
And we hope that our eyes, like the eyes of flies,
will learn to spot movement in the shadows,
against the broken windows.

## THERE IS SOMETHING HUMAN ABOUT
## WANTING TO HOLD A FORK THAT SIZE

I hate your fruit. Someone might
say that. A jolt to the forehead.
What makes the breakdown taste like this?
Your bones are new every eight years.
That your shadow might be shy is an idea.
The key you are waiting to catch. Double
nothing. You think about how you are holding
your hands. Just remember, someone
really loves forks. I describe the fool that falls.
I have a thing, thing. I like things like that.
It's like, *Bird, that piece of bread is too big for you!*
The dancing was good. It was shiny.
Someone might say that. You are funny
sitting over there with your different memories.
No one looks like you when you look like that.
There is a wrong way to be sad. Stop
pointing at me. I am being remarkably funny.
Falling is a common fear. Have you recovered?
It feels like a time to be reasonable. You think.
I think differently.

# HOSTILE AND AGGRESSIVE FEELINGS

Today the barbarian has fifteen minutes
of fame. We think how can we explode this?
Forget it. The barbarian is a fake barbarian.
The barbarian is really a miniature librarian.
Now you are so unhappy. A storytelling of crows.
Generating mistakes. Generating more mistakes.
Geometry is everywhere. I have said of being fine,
*There is good news and there is bad news, though*
*the difference may feel confused.* Illusive perspective.
You do what you don't want to do. You do
what you don't want to do. The results
are stunning and grotesque. It's a gross circus.
It is not an important and enduring legacy.
It's an aggressive loss. Sometimes you scare yourself.
You fear you might be the most ridiculous person
you know. How are your observational skills?
If only it were an exciting experiment.
There was a house. There was a neighbor.
There was a series of distressing and destructive
events. Is the other house being hostile? Houses
fight. Houses fight like giraffes. They stand
side by side facing the same dark street.

# AFTER CALMING DOWN YOU
# HAVE AN OLD FEELING

It's all position position and a push in a
certain direction. We are not calm. A feeling
like the daisies that wouldn't die. It is not
automatic. Then all of a sudden, automatic!
This is an old feeling. A feeling that feels good
now. Like how lions do very cool things
and then are also scary. You can observe this
just after sunset. Just because you know
something doesn't mean someone else does.
When do we learn this? An awareness of
another's awareness. I think you think I think
look at this! Faint sources of light. And water.
Water may exist where you least expect it.
There is water in the lava. The lava like a lion.
Water in the lava. Hydrogen in the hills.
What sort of vision have you had? There is a
heat in my head. The heat comes in distant ships.
How far do you run when you run? There is the
distance between two points. There is the
distance in discussion. There other are distances
too. Are you calm? I am better at hearing
than I am at forgetting.

# ALL OF THE ANIMALS WERE THERE

My name tag reads rabbit. I am
the best refrigerator ever. And other
things. Another thing. A multicellular
organism moving spontaneously.
It's extreme and outrageous and happening
here. Extreme and outrageous conduct
causes a variety of things to maybe happen.
I freak out, freak out, freak out,
with a quiet mouth. Like light breaking
through. Like the wild and precise
thought a hawk has when it sees
an open animal. Here is my hand
shadow of a hawk. A silhouette
is what you see when something
is between you and light. Considerably
simplified. Investigations of this
behavior suggest a lot of nerve.
I keep my fire in the fire. Except
when I don't. You learn a pattern.
You learn another pattern. We're talking
imaginary practice. We're talking
secret parades. Someone says,
*I am drinking water. I'm drinking water again.*
I say, *I want to be a good animal.* What I mean
to say is, *You are exactly where you are
supposed to be.*

# WE ARE HEARING THE LOUDEST
# ANIMAL BE ITS LOUDEST

It's a shrimp. Makes meeting sound like an accident.
A tiger pistol shrimp. Not a whale whistling,
though deaf that might make you. Deep dark
and dangerous feelings are filling our foreheads here.
I remember an airplane to somewhere else.
I was shocking in the restaurant. The deep dark
and dangerous feelings like a different kind of rocket.
The vault alarm alarming. Something good that isn't
recognized at first as such. Such as, when you are mistreated
the same way you mistreat others. And now we are
back to talking about control. I've got a radio in a bucket.
I have a bucket in my hand. What about you? What's in
your hand? A flower. Flowering plants have dominated
the plant scene since dinosaurs and it is a lesson
in perseverance. Yet paleontologists keep changing
their minds just like everyone else. Can you make
yourself completely independent of daylight?
Completely, completely independent. It's the bottom
of the ocean and I will not stop listening to the radio.
It is not mandatory, it's just what I'm doing again today.
Not getting down about the deep dark and dangerous
no daylight. I don't get on the airplane. I get on
the airplane. The airplane smells just like an airplane does.
I cry just like you. And I stop too.

# A NAME THAT HAUNTS YOU
# YOUR NAME THAT HAUNTS YOU

That airplane looked like war. Same sky
a little later a different plane, didn't
look like war. Light refractions making people
see more mystery, more history. The hermit's
roar. An intoxicated feather. Your face.
The feeling of heat appearing to others.
Now my door is red. So many tiny blue dice
fall out of a bottle. You and someone's feelings
not aligning like an unobserved blue. Hands
stained with ink. I think sometimes
we get constrained to expressing immediate
sensations. Subjectivity, symbols and dreams.
Elation or terror. To send a flare signal
on a calm clear day they say to use a flare
that emits bright orange smoke. To send a calm
clear signal on an orange smoke day they say
they say they say

# KEEP YOUR FACE AWAY FROM MY FACE

*Keep your face away from my face*, I sometimes say
in certain circumstances, in very particular situations.
A lap in your head. I have a lot to say about that
but I won't. Sometimes it's just very hard to
know what to do. What to say. Someone
and me are going to the desert. You invite someone.
You invite something. You believe in the world's
best duster kit. I believe bad things are happening
in my head to my eye and I say, *Tibidabo, Tibidabo.*
*Take me back to Tibidabo.* Can we do something
I'm not afraid of? I would like a fact or two maybe.
You have a fact and this comforts the shaking.
It's weird. It's like a glass-eyed animal. It's like
looking with your ear. I had a reason for coming here.
I had a reason for coming here. The reason is elegant
and pulverizing. Like these such circumstances.
Like this situation. Like in the fog when someone yells
and you don't know where the voice is coming from
and the voice is your own.

## TO LEAVE HALF A MIND IS A GIFT
## YOU SOMETIMES GIVE YOURSELF

Nothing I am looking at is moving.
It's believed in order to indicate stability
that one must control one's hand held
here by one's side. The temperament
in your own hand a baby riding a tortoise.
I drew this bear so you would love me
differently. She sang that end for a spider.
For such a night. He kept that mud
hoping to make better. You went that way
to get over there. Real and imagined
faces along and along. A flood in the brain.
We are entering the longest covered bridge.
We are standing in the hottest spot.
In the distance the tallest mountain,
the tallest tree. Further in the distance
the oldest trees, the longest mountain chain.
Nearby the largest lake, the largest cliff.
These ideas do not walk in order to gush.
Like the parts of a clock that regulate
and drive the time we see, there is always
something even smaller going on.
Like how sometimes when you look sad,
people turn away. I was never a horse
with other people. I was only a horse
alone.

# A FOX'S TAIL IS CALLED A BRUSH

There is the room I will pretend does not exist,
for now. For now that room does not exist.
Really remember colors reflected in pools of water.
The marshaling of evidence. Cats of what colors.
A spectrum. Color to describe the cat that is down.
That cat that is to the side. With one eye. What is
scratch made up of? A fluorescent ribosome is working
on figuring it out. Figuring it out in a mouse's mind.
I break up all the leaves into bits. I am hard at summer.
Let the music loud! I can have a color in my mind
and I cannot make it. How do you make a mirror?
I want you to understand. Do you understand me?
I understand. They understand. You understand.
Grasses and radios. Get archaic. A hunter looking
for a streaming blue. You were in the weather.
You idea. A not new idea. A room. I got home
and my door was blue. It was a fox and a picture
of you.

# AN AGREEMENT REQUIRES
# AN OFFER AND ACCEPTANCE

I came here to get you excited.
We have an accidental stare down.
No bees, no money. No one says this.
I am so frightening. No one is impressed.
It's all, a duck's quack doesn't echo
and no one knows why. You think
you are whispering when you are not.
We are experts at distributing distorted
information. This is how it might feel,
take hold of something between
your finger and your thumb and twist it
sharply. Make a slight adjustment.
A logical consequence appears
to arrive, a bar, a partition, a stick.
I am hitting rocks with a stick.
What do you believe to be important
points of convergence? Vegetables.
Electricity. The extremely challenging
sky. To show adoration with the eyes.
To say something necessary. I avoid
my eyes. I think I mean it.

# THE HEART IS MY FAVORITE ORGAN BUT NOT BECAUSE IT IS GRAND

This is what the doctor says. Power and precious
materials. A momentary disruption of consciousness.
The heart will only allow for a moment.
It is concerned with size and size and size. It is
concerned with humors. We are waiting for
the weather. We hope you are not short shelter.
I have some news for the change in my pocket.
Rate, rhythm, axis, interval and wave forms.
In that order often. Knowledge of the immediate
past passing so quickly away. At night outside the train is
another inside of the train. An inevitable process of
adjustment. The conducting system of the heart.
Let's talk about popular astronomy. Your field of vision
a dark area in it. More great stories of ancient lands.
Astronomy lands on your hands. Hands that can
hold how this hurts. Concerned with objects.
An organ is an object. The heart and human affairs
and stars and holes, all concerned with objects.
Calculate a location. Let it linger. I want to drum
that drum.

II.

# BLUE FLAME

Actresses in their dressing rooms,
ambassadors. Undoing distinctions
between body and environment.
A woman standing in the bath.
A woman drying her feet. Reading
after the bath. A lion in the pan.
Not giving a damn about your
demons. Or loving them. Naming
them. Try it with your mouth,
to make a better sound and another
better sound. You start doing it to
stop feeling so much and you keep
doing it to keep feeling so much.

# AFTER VISION

There's a particular recollection
of an event and person. Then there's
what you do or don't do with that.
I tried to tap into the old bitterness
to see if it could teach me anything
about the new bitterness, but it was
a wall. A wall not worth looking at.
Not a wall to walk along. I will. I do
want to believe what I believe about you.
Make up some goodness. Goodness
to hold. Goodness you do hold.
Like a movie. Like a motion picture.
How a motion picture might hold you.
Moving that holds. Some say they want
more clarity. I too want more clarity
and then at other times so much less.
Less clarity that is. You keep pressing
a button like, will this change things?
When does the postman ever ring?
Rings twice. An actress rings when?
The movie makes you cry forever.
How you might think of someone else.

## OBSERVING A TREE YOU ONCE KNEW
## AND NOW NO LONGER KNOW

What can you not take back? What the ears hear
you can't take back. Time cannot be taken back.
I laugh a little and a lot. I cannot take it back.
I am not a horizon. I am a hole. Have a look.
I cannot take it back. They are showing a tree
that represents me. Sometimes you will think, No!
People tell you their stories. Their stories of staring
and standing. Sometimes of serious sadness.
When sadness is in a song it can settle. More
recently evolved structures stacked on top of
older ones. If the smoke keeps the people
away, ok. It's a noise a bug is making in the dark.
That's like that. There are records. Here's a record.
The town touches me too much. I have taken time here.
I cannot take it back. For your window I would be a
willow. Trees tend to grow in clusters. Take this
into consideration. I cannot take it back. Realism
and variety.

# IDEA

I want the engine. I invent a machine,
I mean engine. My map this mess, trying
to make the most of many things. We have
tried to find some things. You, the town is small
and our eyes are smaller! Bright plants,
these are arrows with weight. The signs
that glass and calm. This is about shapes and
positions. Planet-hunting instruments. If you want
to paint a ceiling so that it looks far away
how do you paint it so? To be a random wind-
storm. The door across the street opens.
We have been careful with you. As quiet as
the snow. And then, even quieter. The tiniest
spiders have brains extending into their legs.
Brains in your legs! You let someone learn
to like it. You need not know what it means.
Like the idea that if you are touching someone
you know someone is there.

# YOU KEEP ASKING WHAT I WANT
# AND I DON'T KNOW WHAT I WANT

A million different landscapes with snow.
It's a study of bees. These are your future ducks.
We get desperate. We start dancing. It is a weird
come apart. No returns of cake. No exchanges
of cake. Run your thumb across your bottom lip.
Run your thumb across your bottom lip again.
I float quietly. I have a nice stand. I don't know
how to say, I'm just looking. We breathe air.
We keep the same body temperature all day.
We are holding onto things. An unspecified
racket. A small wagon. The biggest warehouse.
It's ambitious and complicated. It's a result
that is still unclear and can go either way.
I do not know what I have to make. I make
mistakes and many of them. I'm afraid I make
many mistakes. This has something to do
with the desperation and something to do
with other things too. A web of smoke holding
onto a dark night. Refusing to reflect any light.
Tell me things. I am waiting for you to tell me things.
I want you to tell me things.

# THE OPPOSITION OF OBJECTS

There was no figuring it out. We just wanted
to make a thing. Make another thing. Oranges.
Yellows you see and see. Representations of animals
living in mountains, swamps, rivers, oceans, and
barnyards. In the town, in the city. There's the bus
we ride. There's the train we ride. There's the boat.
The plane. We saw someone change someone
else's life. Watched that mean something.
Thought that seemed something. What is the word
for that sort of geography? The sound of a bell.
A pleasantly sharp taste. Madness. Knitting.
Heads. Fascinating. We couldn't make it a picture
that made sense. The snow looks almost like sound.
Sand. Sand almost sounds like sound. They present
spaces in our hearts we hadn't heard before. They
were spaces in our hearts we hadn't heard before.

# BUG

The frustration you feel is like a
puddle of water you don't want to step in
but cannot avoid stepping in. Of course
perhaps you can avoid it and at this time
it is simply unfortunate that you are convinced
you cannot. You are a bug crawling up an arm.
You are the look of shame a face cannot displace
upon being what we sometimes call, caught.
Groundhog, you do not wear the dead
flowers like a boss. Trap got you.
The dude that keeps repeating, *Timeless*
*timeless timeless.* Eyes that roll over
and over. Back to the bug. There are
like a billion kinds.

# THEY WILL CALL YOU
# DIFFERENT THINGS

Strange. Odd. Unknown.
Occasional. Nonsense.
Deviant. Flickering. A circle.
A wheel. A cycle. The uncertain.
I walk an inventory of colors.
Wave. Ocean. Open water.
I collect an inventory of colors
but I cannot remember them.
I over and over again forget them.
Collect them and then forget them.
Collect them and then forget them.
Someone recalls something
about Isaac Newton. How
do you know a color? A prism.
A dark room. The right angle.
The sun saying something.
The blue light leading to the idea
of light as a thing. A walk along
water. New and opposite thoughts.
Eyes closed. An observation.
The sea saying, *See how nothing
stays the same?*

# INDIGNANT

I wanted you to be addressing me.
I wanted what you were saying to be
about me. I am wearing a dress
sometimes. Wearing a dress is a way
I have been described. Dude man,
I don't want your dress. I have my own.
You don't describe me. You don't say.
Now I'm just being silly. Or so you say.
Being silly is a way I have been described.
You don't know me. And yet, what you said
is trying to claim that you know me. No.
It is easy to forget you can say something
after saying it and saying it and no one
hearing you say it. Displacement
with the everything. Everything occurring
at once. I get goose bumps. I am a gone
goose. You can't say boo to a goose.
Boo. Seriously. Respect a fly.

# WATER I HAVE SEEN A DUCK

I cannot imagine life continuing with the bird.
*Bird be better*, I say. I am trying to be better.
Recognizing and correcting one's imperfections.
This filament does not work. This filament does
not work. And then and then and then an instant
of discovery. I feel pain in my dreams. Do you
feel pain in your dreams? The fixed look of touch
water wears when moved by wings or other
things. I don't want to withhold my admiration
but it is hard to photograph the rain.

# THE FEAR OF AN ACCELERATING SOMETHING

A trailer, a pyramid. A road that travelers take.
What someone wants is for you to believe
in that someone. Someone. In the shade to stammer.
Omitted but understood. I take my postcards
to the post office. I take my suitcase to the station.
My boat is moving away from your boat. My boat
to an edge. Your boat to a different edge. How many
edges does a pyramid have? It depends on the number
of sides the pyramid has. The processing power of a brain
that might lead eyes to see buildings that look like boats.
Conflicting information collected. Calibrating one's certainty
level to the strength of evidence, of enduring uncertainty
for long stretches of time. To see transportation
as transformation. Subtraction to tell time. Associations
of opposites. Associations of sound. To remember
is a sort of repetition. Do I want to remember?
What to remember.

# FAMILIAR QUALITIES WE ADMIRE

To be praiseworthy and principled.
To be kind and caring. To be perfectly
daring. What if you could sense a magnetic
field? An electrical field? Some animals can.
To recognize magic as magic. It's time-
sensitive. Your sensory input of stimuli
tells you one thing and your basis of
knowledge tells you another. It is good
that some astronauts love David Bowie.
I am eating a biscuit very slowly. Drinking
the old water. It's over a billion years old.
The recognition training a broken photograph.
Another airplane. Cool, smart, and nice
are commonly used ways to describe someone
likable. Seems simple listed like that.
Draw a circle. Draw a line. Draw another line.
Draw a triangle. I said to do these things.
Do these things. Now explain how to
do these things.

# PANIC

I had a lack of legs. I, a tiny problem.
For cameras, see concealed cameras.
For chessboard, see cigarette. For
microdots, see microdots. For pencil,
for pipe, for playing card, see ring.
For self-destruction of, for shoe, stamp,
walnut, see cows. Just explaining.
Not taking a position. Someone says,
*The temporal bone is the most difficult bone*
*in the body.* Someone says, *It is the most*
*intimidating bone in the body.* The temporal
bone making moments all along the ear canal.
Another animal was making a noise
and for the longest time I think it is
the animal that is me. Animals with ancient
names occupy a ship in another book
of real inventory. Not the book I took
for taking pictures. I am panicking. I am
panicking. And the book I took says,
*for escape equipment, see the eye.*

# LEGO LADY YOU HAVE TWO HEADS

Is the world library a giant cat?
Is the future innocent?
Entanglements are like tiny drugs.
Watermelon. Unripe please.
Commercials are not illegal but
sometimes tiny. It's a program.
To protect yourself back up.
Money in a bucket. It's not
going to look like a beach.
I watch television very slowly.
Bending can act like a lens. Any area
of the tongue can pick up taste.
A moderately bright star.
When it's no use going to the sea
I tend to. What is happening
at this hotel? Statistics are funny.
15 percent to 20 percent of many
species are watchful. To keep
ahead of the watching and the wind
and the water. So and so said this.
Say that. Here it is raining like
Spring! I am something if you say so.
Say so.

# TINY

I look for a tree with a big hole
in it. I like tiny things. Scale calls us
to pay attention in particular ways.
Huge thunderclaps, hard to find cloud.
A private investigator that I don't know
endorses me for having a skill that
I hope I have. I have no idea why
this private investigator does this.
Waves traveling in shallow water.
Waves that have traveled long distances.
I get down at too many interchanges. I worry
I am always in the way. I'm in the way
of this wave. How can you be in the way
of a wave? How can you be tiny and in
the way? The wave is like, *You can be tiny*
*and in the way like you can be big enough*
*to build something bigger than yourself.*

# THAT THAT THAT

I look at the pictures over and over.
To help me remember. We did that
and we did this. He did that. Covered
in leaves. She did that. They did that.
Salt in the water. I did that. Elk by
the side of the road. The elk by the side
of the road alive. You by the side of
the road alive. The calendar is impatient.
Borges explains it in his story with
the character who wants to name
everything. Wants all new numbers.
Wants one word for everything and anything.
I want to be an orange ball of music.
Could you hear me sewing in the dark?
Finishing something.

# III.

# HANDS LIKE LIGHTERS

I would just light the fire
& forget it.
I would just light the fire
& forget it.
I would just light the fire
& forget it.
I don't want to, didn't want to
talk about it.


\*


I look up *contrition*. It's up in the air like
legs. I moved my legs, moved my legs,
moved my legs.

Look at how you are moving your legs.
And look

almost maybe nothing

was said.


\*


Say, was that ok?

I do want to dance.
I want to dance.
I would maybe.

*

You are air or something.
But for a second,
you think you are water.

Where does the wanting
water come from?

*

Hands like lighters.
No, not like lighters,
Lighters.

*

Hands like lighters.
No, not like lighters,
Lighters.

\*

No amount of fire enough.
No amount of earth enough.
No amount of water enough.

I hope enough air might get me there.
There where I want to be.

\*

I want words and what seems like
endless patience. A mile crashing you
in and out.

You said you just want me
to sit next to you.
To hold your hand.
These shapes.

\*

Hands like lighters.
No, not like lighters,
Lighters.

\*

To wish, to find, to surrender, to appear, to descend, to see, to know, to show, to wait, to say, to run, to temper, to flee, to steal, to absorb, to ring, to read, to make, to feel, to hear, to tell, to watch, to wake, to consider, to deliver.

\*

Concerned with articulation
of that which is beyond
what is perceptible to some
of the senses.

Simultaneously a sponge
and a projector.

See how you saw those silhouettes
and in so seeing saw a certain way
to work well against a wall?

\*

I have a wall and you're too tall
not to see around it. Air above.
You have those eyes. These eyes

above me. What is the word
for their shape?


*


The shape
of shame
is super
shifting.

Or is it stuck?


*


Hands like lighters.
No, not like lighters,
Lighters.


*


Hands like lighters.
No, not like lighters,
Lighters.

\*

The shape of shame
colliding with the old somethings.

You can't explain what you want
to explain because you are worried
it won't make any sense.

\*

Water and toast.
Water and toast.
Water and toast.

Water and toast.

Water and toast.
Water and toast.
Water and toast.

Water and toast.
Water and toast.

\*

Hands like lighters.
No, not like lighters,
Lighters.


*


There are certain things
that it wouldn't make sense
to say we did.

In the new diagram
nothing was buried
or what was buried
wasn't buried below.

Below the ground that is.


*


Mostly I look like this
by accident.

Mostly I do want
to look at you.

*

Do you want to
look at me?

*

Hands like lighters.
No, not like lighters,
Lighters.

*

Casual lighthouses
are what we want to be.

But lighthouses aren't
casual.

*

The person stops being a person.

The person becomes the idea of _____ .

The idea of pain.

*

Hands like lighters.
No, not like lighters,
Lighters.

*

Hands like lighters.
No, not like lighters,
Lighters.

*

I am having trouble breathing again.

You, the one I love, live for yourself.

It can be hard to look at.

It can be a lot to love.

*

I get reckless and down.
It's internal but out there.


*


When do you like to dance?


*


The nature is that there is no story.
No way to make what happened a story.


*


You have stories.
You dance.


*

It feels hard to fuck up a rock,
so you think
be a rock.


But you can't be.

So you dance.

You dance maybe.

Spirals to an edge.


*


Hands like lighters.
No, not like lighters,
Lighters.


*


Words can't describe the wound.

Perhaps more importantly words alone
can't heal the wound.

\*

I love words.
I thought I hated bodies.

I didn't know I could love
a body.

I didn't know I could let
somebody love my body.

\*

To have, to think, to unlink, to take, to presume, to reach, to plan, to land, to break, to help, to wait, to work, to make, to know, to read, to prepare, to remember, to hold.

\*

Hands like lighters.
No, not like lighters,
Lighters.

\*

So it seemed sense was going
to have to change.

That what to arrange
might not be words.

*

We are so much water.

We are so often wanting to dance.

And you, you are air too.

*

How do you hold a body
of air?

How do you let go
of the idea of the word *fair*?

*

Hands like lighters.
No, not like lighters,
Lighters.

\*

To hope, to give, to watch, to wish, to leave, to call, to fall, to open, to see, to collect, to circle, to long, to know, to go, to stretch, to allow, to reflect, to need, to forgive, to undo, to imagine, to want, to touch, to crash, to loose, to hear, to change.

\*

I was waiting for it to rain hard
like this.

I was going to change hard
like this.